LONELINESS TO BE LOVED

HARITHA AARUMUGAM

Copyright © Haritha Aarumugam
All Rights Reserved.

For my Grandmother,

Maasilamani Ramasamy

Contents

Contents

Acknowledgements

Compiling this book would not be possible without the input of many. I would like to thank all of them who supported and make it as the product. My particular gratitude goes to:

All the magnificent poets Genita, Haneesh L, Naveen Prasanth, Reshmi S, Dharani K, Gayathri M, Harshini M, Keerthi, Thanu Sree and Indhu, who placed their outstanding poems.

Notion Press, my publisher for offering me an opportunity.

Genita Gladys, my editor for deftly editing the book and also loving it.

Aarumugam and Latha, my parents, I am indebted to them for all the love that surrounds me.

My Family and Friends, for their unconditional love and encouragement.

Last but not least, You, the reader, for the leap of faith in picking up this book.

1.My Forever Love

In all the cases; who fake a promise

You are the only soul who

Drizzle with love

You endure all the pains; I give you

Words can't explain this fairytale is-

'My forever love!'

One Life; One Love; Only you.

-Harry Sree

2.Bourgeoisie

"Indebted" - God

For my validation

Longed for a sunrise;

Knucle down before dawn

Hankered bon appétit;

Had a despondency hit

"Map out a voyage"

Just trek in this cage

Yearned to be "Ms. Tween"

"my childhood" - disreagarded

God - Ain't I impugn,

He Slurred "Bourgeoisie".

-Genita Gladys

3.Breeze

How gaily the wind whistled in my ears!

Or turning my face towards the sky;

I would absorb it's shining radiance and blue into my soul,

That Opened wide to welcome it.

-Harry Sree

4.My Heart

That daring look gave me chills

Innocent smile made my days

Sweet talk made my way

Being with you made me whole

Your caring thought revs my heart

My problem is heart and the solution is you

You are that part of me I'll always need..

-Haneesh L

5.Mind Of Love

Even I close my eyes

I'm scattering in your smile;

Not today--

but I hope the days will unite us

and I'll wait, for you…

That moment you'll be,

ready to accept me

Cause I'll make my confession.

-Harry Sree

6.Dear Fairy

I'll kiss you gently,

Caz you mine queen,

Dear mine love me more,

Caz you, more than my soul.

Princess make all as possible,

The peace I feel I can't express,

One can't always with you,

Possible, You the great.

O you the strongest one here,

I'll never leave you any cost,

Five plus years a break,

Tone makes worthy Five,

Waiting tone, waiting for tone.

-Naveen Prasanth

7.Heart of Smile

If someone tackle you-

Hold them in your smile

Let them, break grudge.

If they smile at you-

Make freshen with bloom

Cause Smile is lark.

Which non's life has failed to park

Not everyone holding in grudge

Grudge itself; hide in smile

-Harry Sree

8.Fallen Flower

Was a flower in your tree,

Waiting for you to notice,

But forgot there were thousand more;

Wishing you'd pick me,

Slapped by the fast breeze,

Fell on the ground heart-broken,

Then, found myself touching you,

But under your shoes,

For a brief moment,

I was at heaven,

Got to know I'll be there forever.

-Reshmi.S

9. The World Of Fantasy

Thankyou for showing me

"The world of fantasy"

I saw unclear pearls-

My hands filled with Crystals,

Sometimes unwittingly sharpened-

And hopeful prophecy:

On the other hand you might be boon

Where everyone love to be with you

You made--thy happier, happier:

And Happier.

-Harry Sree

10.Certified Mortal

Be a deaf..

So that you can't hear a backbiting,

Be a dumb..

So that you can't speak unripe words,

Be a blind..

So that you can't spot an injustice and walkaway,

Be heartless..

So that you can't be stone hearted.

-Dharani.K

11. Lament to Her

The day which I want to hide,

The day which I failed to fight--for you at very last moment

The day which you left me with blindfold

The day which I lost you;

The day where I spent the whole day with you,

And that became the final day.

By seconds, you become stronger in me and

I'm starting to miss you A lot

When can I reach you - that

I am able to sleep on your lap for a while

-Harry Sree

12.Nature

Rain drops falling Down

Droplets glitters in the colour of Crown

Affords enthusiastic feel to the whole Town

It washed away all our Mourn

Feel the breezy Air

Whatever happens don't Care

Today admiring nature is very Rare

Understand nature is a unique Flair.

-Gayathri.M

13.Gusting Wind

The raging wind that sways me away

Wit full throttle moving in the highway

Driving like a ship in the sea storm

Heat of the machine makes me warm

With the power of will that never bends

Feeling of the journey never ends

...

-Harry Sree

14. The Everlasting of Father's Love

I hold your hands,

I saw the entire world.

The affection of you is time everlasting,

Be that as it may, something made me to misfortune you.

Miss you a ton my world

Father is a gift from God.

Father's affection is a time everlasting,

Love you appa,

I miss you appa.

-Harshini.M

15.Faultless Pal

No more dream I have:

Holding hands together

We make a life happier

Behind us…

Can I make a part alike

That can't be a making alive:

Not here,

We can't stop here; Yeah bae it's a friend

Who friend in need ,She never be apart

In my heart,

Who always bear my patience

At a very end.

-Harry Sree

16.Pleasure

I shared my pain with others

For years,

And ended with more pain,

Five minute of self-talk was enough to

Release my pain,

And reduce my strain.

-Keerthi

17.Am I "The One"

Am I — "The one"

Am I the one who belongs to you?

Am imprisoned in her eyes

Where could I survive my life??

Is this—"The Last"

Is this my last breath?

No I want to live the fullest.

I found her heart, which has love for me

And care for me,

Even in my dreams-Even in my death,

I'm falling for her…

Am I the one who falling for her?

-Harry Sree

18.Senior Pal Of Mine

Don't tell her that she'sshort

Still carries herself like a fine art!

She was out-of-place for days

My eyes pursued in all the ways!

I've fallen between crack

And It's her who got me in track!

The sole senior who has my heart

Oh Lord! Ever let us apart!

All I wish to stay beside her!

And that's my ultimate desire!

-Thanu Sree

19. Thinking Of You

Thinking of you, makes me fly

Over the sky to reach you;

I feel the world in my hands

While thinking of you;

Anywhere, everywhere, forever- I'm thinking of you

I'm thinking of you.

Do you feel my love?

-Harry Sree

20.I'm Yours

I thought God created my life-for 'You',

But not:

Your Eyes, the fire of Sun and Victory over moon.

God blessed my life just to surrender in those rays

And, I don't want to be rescued from it.

I don't care about the four parts:

Walls, Directions, Talks and Lives,

Because I'm yours.

-Harry Sree

21.Dearest Floret!

Dearest Floret! Bloom! As deity;

I am surrendered to God's heart, Who created you.

World celebrate your aristocracy,

I'm bowing your Royalty Elite Empresses jealousy;

Let the Nation fallen.

Not for formality, But for dignity

My love took you to me;

I feel your warm smile.

My dearest Darling, Waiting for you…

Just to cross our fingers;

My love for you. Elite our lives,

Let my love take you to me

I wanna see your warmer smile

I don't like to bow others,

But I am surrendered to God's heart

Who created you.

-Harry Sree

22.Gentle Dame

Am I one?"

Traveling with you

Made Life Mystery:

Searching for you,

Never stopped ubiquitously.

Longing for you,

with bowing heads

started turning felicity.

Rebirthing my life,

On your eyes.

Gifted my hands

Like Santa Claus

Filled With feathers,

Filled with flowers

Still you excelling.

-Harry Sree

23.Wrinkled Us

By move on sweating Drizzle over the field,

It raptured everyone eyes.

Sixty passed summer and winter

The arms of you never faded,

Not having exhausted but you.

Shedding flowers beautified because of you,

Scrutinize smell of rain Premature spilled their hilarity.

Wrinkled infant reminiscing last day,

Let me born one more; To tie up with your company,

Again hold off palms together.

Bliss of mine overwhelmed

Enjoyed one which longed-for…

Like Romeo, Everyone wears mask

Is bayonet or weary..??

-Harry Sree

24.Ruptured with Her Thoughts

Look at her smile, how can I get back it?

Strayed euphrosyne, where can I go?

Missed iambe, where can I search?

Misplaced venus, where can I recover it?

Lost wayward, where can I survive?

She parted, how can I apologize??

-Harry Sree

25.Blissfull Adieu

He awaited for he;

She gone for him.

We longed for their love;

Even felt happy for their accomplishment

They both got the park of heaven.

-Harry Sree

26. You Believe

You Believe in knowledge,

When things happen what you thought,

You Believe in hope,

When things does not happen what you though.

You Believe in god,

When unexpected things happen,

You Believe in wisdom,

When expected things happen,

You believe in fate,

When talent becomes useless.

You start believing in yourself,

When you realize that you are

The only strength of your own

Knowledge, hope, wisdom and fate.

-Indu

27.Attitude

An epic estimated towards her eyes

Dark and white combined epic

Open and closing symbolized majestic:

We have the priority of our lives

Once you struck up with my emotions

You will strike up with my pauses…

-Harry Sree

28.Let Her Eyes Capture Us

Hold the catchers,

Bold the streamers,

Mold the dreamers,

Fold the stars,

Let her eyes capture us.

-Harry Sree

29.Unknown Me

I ran out of my life faraway from distrace;

to escape entire strife.

However days mislead

my work continued; to secure my appetite.

Suddenly, I searched a voice

which annoyed me,

every moment to make farce.

Missing warm hugs,

delightful laughs,

entrusted eyes;

I made a mistake

I should reborn apace;

With all my love.

-Harry Sree

30.My Child Birth

At dusk morning,

A grass having drop

Faded away while seeing

My child's first drop.

-Harry Sree